GW00568213

Opening Combination Padlocks

NO TOOLS, NO PROBLEM

CARL BLACK

PALADIN PRESS · BOULDER, COLORADO

Opening Combination Padlocks: No Tools, No Problem
by Carl Black

Copyright © 2002 by Carl Black

ISBN 13: 978-1-58160-368-2
Printed in the United States of America

Published by Paladin Press, a division of
Paladin Enterprises, Inc.
Gunbarrel Tech Center
7077 Winchester Circle
Boulder, Colorado 80301, USA
+1.303.443.7250

Direct inquiries and/or orders to the above address.

Visit our Web site at: www.paladin-press.com

Table of Contents

Warning

The author, publisher, and distributors of this book in no way endorse or condone any potentially illegal activity or act and disclaim any liability for the use or misuse of the information contained herein. This book is *for information purposes only*.

# Introduction

I have always found locksmithing to be a fascinating trade, or should I say art. The various types of locks, their properties, and a general understanding of their inner workings have always intrigued me. I spend countless hours tearing apart and reassembling any and every new lock I can get my hands on to obtain as much knowledge as possible on how and why they work.

What has interested me the most, however, is the actual manipulation of locks. Being able to open a lock by unconventional or irregular means is quite an exciting thing. Just knowing that you have the skill to gain access—if desired—is an invigorating feeling. The information in this book is obviously not intended to be used in a foul or illegal manner, but rather to educate those with the same passion for unorthodox and exotic information that I hunger after.

The following pages will explain in detail what I believe to be the quickest and most effective method to open any combination padlock. It will also explain why and how it works, and give problem-solving aids should any complications arise.

I have read various books on combination padlock manipulation, some better than others. However, after reading these books I just was not satisfied. Some techniques did not allow entry into all locks, other techniques made it very difficult or confusing to always accurately find the 1st or 3rd number, which was usually the main basis for their technique. These systems usually involved some means of pulling out on the shackle while trying to recognize the number/gate with the least resistance when the dial was moved back and forth. I always found this to be a difficult method because if you initially incorrectly determined the number/gate you were in for a lot of useless and time-consuming effort.

For these reasons I decided to devise a foolproof system that would allow the quickest and most efficient entry into all combination padlocks without any guesswork. By knowing the inner workings of the lock and its specific traits and properties I was able to come up with a very easily learned formula that I have found no other manipulation technique can match. Once learned and practiced, you should be able to determine the combination of a padlock in minutes. I am certain that once you've finished reading this book and tried my system that you will be more than satisfied with its results.

Other books on opening padlocks also seem to try to appear as conventional aids in the locksmithing trade. They go into drilling, picking, reading open locks, code books, etc. Well, my thoughts on the subject are:

1. If you want to learn the actual locksmithing trade, go to school or take a course.

2. If the lock is already open, why would you need to read it?

3. Have you ever tried picking a combination padlock? The resistance between the shackle and body is so tight on today's combination locks it makes it practically impossible to force any type of shim into the lock between them.

4. If you've got combination codebooks, why do you need to read a book on manipulation?

5. If you are going to drill the back of the lock, you are already compromising its integrity and you might as well cut the shackle.

Therefore, I have written this book with the sole purpose of teaching one thing and one thing only—the best overall method of manipulating a combination padlock. How you decide to apply your new knowledge on the subject is entirely up to you (as long as it is not used in an illegal manner, of course).

Examining the Lock

Throughout this discussion we will be using an American Lock padlock as our main reference lock. There are various other types of padlocks of course: Master Lock, PM, Brinks, Excel, Hampton, etc. Padlocks by American have fewer gates, as will be explained later, and will thus be easier to get started with and practice on.

Figure 1 shows a cross section of a disassembled American lock. Keep in mind that different lock brands and manufacturers are going to have slightly different designs and internal hardware. The overall function of these different designs, however, will all work in a similar manner that will not have any significant effect on the manipulation technique covered.

One of the best pieces of advice that I can give to anyone interested in lock picking or manipulation is to get to know the lock on a personal basis. Tear it apart and play with it; see for yourself all the pieces and parts and exactly how they work together to operate. Without this visual reference point you are at a great disadvantage. Now, I am not saying that this must be done in order for my method to work; it will work regardless. However, a strong mental picture of what is going on inside while you are working outside is priceless. This knowledge will become useful should any complications arise, as will be explained later. So once again, I strongly suggest that you disassemble a lock or two and become acquainted with them as much as possible.

Those who are somewhat ignorant on lock picking and have watched too many movies may be under the impression that one can open a combination lock merely by putting one's ear to the lock and listening to the clicking noises made while turning the dial. This I would pay to see. An average combination lock has approximately 64,000 different combinations. Breaking down the number of different combination possibilities will be a main focus of our manipulation technique.

Did you ever notice that when you quickly dialed the combination on your wall locker in high school, or any padlock for that matter, it still opened even though you were a number or so off? There is a reason it still opened. When you look at the dial of your lock, it shows numbers 0 through 39. Unlike a safe, vault, or some other more expensive or complicated lock, the combination padlocks we are exploring do not actually have 40 different numbers, or what we will refer to as "gates." They will usually only have 10 or 12 gates, instantly diminishing the number of possible combinations.

While examining your disassembled lock (see Figure 2), notice the gates that we are referring to. Each gate is separated by a small, raised notch, with one gate being cut out. The gate that has the opening cut out is the true gate; the rest are false gates. If you inspect wheels #1 and #2 (Fig. 1), you will notice a space cut out of them as well, similar to that of the true gate. As you could deduce, when all three of these gates are aligned under the lever, it allows an opening for the lever to fall into when you pull up on the shackle, thus opening the lock.

Using the American padlock in Figure 2 as our example, we find that it has 10 gates—nine false gates and one true gate. So instead of having 40 numbers, as the dial would indicate, in actuality we are only dealing with 10. (Each gate represents four numbers on the dial, which is why the lock will open even if you are a number or so off.)

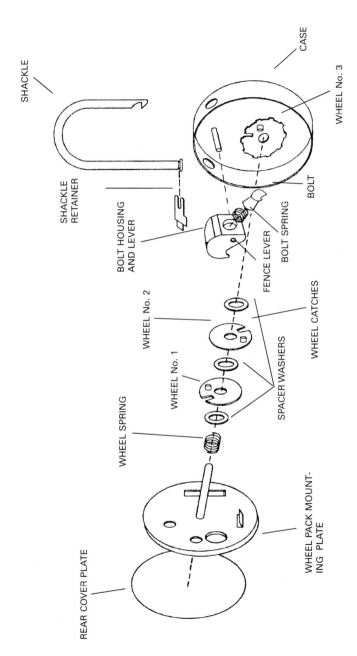

Figure 1: Exploded view of a generic combination padlock.

Lock
Principles

There are several standard principles of combination pad-locks that need to be understood. Some are very basic and others will be part of the basis for our formula/technique. Obtain as sound a grasp and understanding of them as possible, as these six principles will be referred to periodically throughout the rest of the manuscript.

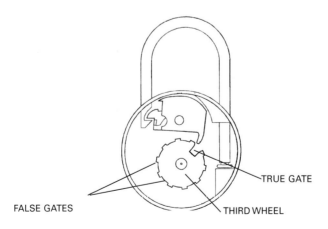

Figure 2: Rear view (cutaway) of a 10-gate lock.

Principle 1: All combinations are right-left-right.

Principle 2: You must initially turn the dial clockwise at least two full rotations to the right before stopping at the first number. This basically ensures that all wheels have been caught and are spinning and that the previous combination attempt has been erased. (Don't make this seem complicated; you have always given the dial a quick spin or two before starting in on your combination, now you just know why you were doing it.)

Principle 3: The second number in the combination will be at least one full turn to the left past the first number, and at least four numbers less than the first number. This may also sound complicated but it isn't; quick example: if the first number is 20, then after you stop at 20 you have to make at least one full rotation left back past 20, and the second number will be somewhere between 21 and 16 rotating counterclockwise. So you know the second number cannot be 17, 18, 19, or 20. Again, simply because of another mechanical quality of the lock, the combination possibilities have decreased in our favor. The extent of the benefits of this principle will be explained when we start our manipulation technique.

Principle 4: The third number will be less than one full turn to the right of the second number. It will *usually* be at least four numbers less than the second number. This is basically a repeat of Principle 3. If the second number is 10, then after you stop at 10 and start rotating back right, the third number will be somewhere between 9 and 14 rotating clockwise. So the third number will most likely not be 13, 12, 11, or 10.

Principle 5: The combination of numbers will *usually* be low-high-low or high-low-high. This means that the first and second number, or the second and third number will *usually* not be extremely close together. For example, have you ever had a lock combination of 21-22-23 or 2-3-4? I'm not saying that the numbers are always evenly spaced, but the probability of the first and second number or the second and third number being within four to eight numbers or one or two gates (as you will soon learn) is a lot lower. By exploiting the flaws and weaknesses of the lock we are able to use a sort of refined probability analysis to, again, substantially decrease the combination possibilities of the lock.

Principle 6: Once you have stopped at the second number and started to rotate back to the right, you can begin pulling out on the shackle (to locate the third number or final gate) without disrupting the position of the first two wheels.

Principle 6 will play an important role in substantially cutting the time required to work through the remaining combination possibilities and open the lock. Again, this may sound complicated but really is not. Do not let this or any other principle start to confuse or intimidate you; you do not have to be a rocket scientist to use the manipulation technique that I am about to explain. I simply wanted to go into as much detail as possible in order to give you the greatest amount of knowledge and understanding of the lock, its characteristics, and the foundation of laws and theories supporting this technique in relation to how and why it works.

The Manipulation Technique

All right, let's get to it. The items that you will need:

A combination padlock
A pen or pencil
A piece of paper

The first thing that needs to be done is to find the gates (refer to Figure 2). Though this can be quickly and easily accomplished, it is a very critical step and requires your attention to detail and accuracy. This can most easily be done by holding the lock in your right hand (if you are right-handed, or whatever is most comfortable), inserting the ring and middle finger of your left hand in the shackle opening and applying an upward force or pressure on the shackle. I recommend starting with the dial on 0 for simplicity.

While pulling up on the shackle try to move the dial back and forth with your right hand. You should be able to feel a slight friction when turning; this is the lever rubbing on the bottom of the gate. You should also only be able to turn the dial one or two numbers before its movement is blocked on both sides. These are the two sides of the gate, which separate it from the next gates.

Some locks will require more or less pull to lower the lever within the gate far enough for you to be able to feel where the gate begins and ends. Tools like vice grips and pipe wrenches shouldn't be needed. If for some reason you are not able to locate the gates no matter how much force you exert, or if you are only able to find one gate, don't give up hope. I will show you some techniques to overcome these dilemmas later on in your reading.

After pulling up on the shackle and rotating the dial back and forth you should have located the first gate. Now, as you are rotating the dial back and forth, look at the numbers that the dial stops at on both sides. With the American lock we are using, the gate walls should be two numbers apart. For illustration, we'll say that the dial's left and right limits are 0 and 2. The centermost point of these limits is what we are after. This will give us the most accurate location of the center of the gate, allowing the least amount of friction and chance of hitting the edge of the gate due to human error when plugging in the combination. So if our first gate started at 0 and stopped at 2, then 1 would put us right in the middle of the gate.

(However, it is possible that your gate starts and stops between two numbers. For example, say it started between the 0 and 1 and stopped at 2½. Not a problem, the same rule applies. Your first gate would still be halfway between the two numbers—1½.)

We will use the example of 1 as our first gate for simplicity. Record your first gate number (1) on the top of your sheet of paper. Now, slightly release the tension on the shackle while slowly turning the dial to the left. Continue to turn the dial to the left until you feel the lever bypassing the right gate wall and entering the next gate. Since this lock has 10 gates, the next gate should be approximately four numbers to the right of the first gate.

Once you have located the position of the second gate, again apply upward tension on the shackle while rotating the dial back and forth to find its left and right limits. We find these limits to be 4 and 6. Once again we want to find the centermost point of this gate, which is again halfway between the left and right limits (4 and 6), giving us 5 as our second gate. Record this number to the right of your first number. Continue this process all the way around the dial until you reach your initial starting point. You should have 10 numbers recorded on your paper as shown:

1-5-9-13-17-21-25-29-33-37

If the gates landed on a half number as previously described, that list of numbers should look as follows:

1½-5½-9½-13½-17½-21½-25½-29½-33½-37½

As you were finding the gates, you more than likely noticed the gate numbers you recorded were all four numbers apart. You probably asked yourself why you had to waste the time finding the remaining gates when an established pattern had evolved and you knew they would all be four numbers apart. Good question—technically you did not. However, I recommend manually finding every gate if you have not had the experience before. After you get the hang of it though, once you have accurately found the first few gates and know how many gates the lock has, there really is no reason you cannot plug in the remaining gate numbers to save time.

As stated earlier, this is a very quick and simple part of the process. You should be able to determine and record the gate numbers in less than a minute. At the same time, you want to ensure your records of the gate center locations are accurate. As with anything manufactured by machines, there is always a chance for error. These errors could cause a gate to be cut slightly smaller or larger than it should be. This is one reason I recommend determining each gate manually. Accurately determining the gate center locations will relieve a lot of time being wasted later in the process.

Once you have recorded the gate numbers, the next step is to simply complete the table of combination possibilities. Start with the first number (1) and directly beneath it copy down the other gate numbers in order. Next, do the same for your second gate number (5) following the same technique as before. Continue this process until the entire table is completed, as shown in Table 1.

This table represents all the first- and second-number combination possibilities for the lock. The top row shows first-number possibilities and the row of numbers beneath them are the second-number possibilities.

The next thing we need to do is start breaking down the number of combination possibilities as far as we can. This can be done by using the lock principles, probability, and deductive reasoning. Looking at Principle 3, we find we can completely eliminate the last row of numbers as second-number possibilities. Referring to Principle 5, we can determine the probability of the second number being one gate from the first number to be extremely low. This allows us to tentatively eliminate the first row of second-number possibilities. Again, by using Principle 5 and the laws of probability, we can reasonably deduce that the chance of the second number being within two gates of the first number in either direction is also extremely low. We can then tentatively cross out the second and next-to-last row of second-number possibilities.

1st No. Possibilities

1	5	9	13	17	21	25	29	33	37
5	9	13	17	21	25	29	33	37	1
9	13	17	21	25	29	33	37	1	5
13	17	21	25	29	33	37	1	5	9
17	21	25	29	33	37	1	5	9	13
21	25	29	33	37	1	5	9	13	17
25	29	33	37	1	5	9	13	17	21
29	33	37	1	5	9	13	17	21	25
33	37	1	5	9	13	17	21	25	29
37	1	5	9	13	17	21	25	29	33

2nd No. Possibilities

TABLE 1

Opening Combination Padlocks

1st No. Possibilities

1	5	9	13	17	21	25	29	33	37
~~5~~	~~9~~	~~13~~	~~17~~	~~21~~	~~25~~	~~29~~	~~33~~	~~37~~	~~1~~
~~9~~	~~13~~	~~17~~	~~21~~	~~25~~	~~29~~	~~33~~	~~37~~	~~1~~	~~5~~
13	17	21	25	29	33	37	1	5	9
17	21	25	29	33	37	1	5	9	13
21	25	29	33	37	1	5	9	13	17
25	29	33	37	1	5	9	13	17	21
29	33	37	1	5	9	13	17	21	25
~~33~~	~~37~~	~~1~~	~~5~~	~~9~~	~~13~~	~~17~~	~~21~~	~~25~~	~~29~~
~~37~~	~~1~~	~~5~~	~~9~~	~~13~~	~~17~~	~~21~~	~~25~~	~~29~~	~~33~~

MOST PROBABLE 2nd #'s

TABLE 2

Each first number is now left with five second-number combination possibilities, for a total of 50 total combination possibilities. We will call this group of numbers our "sweet spot"—the numbers having the highest possibility of being the second number. Table 2 shows a revised table with the most probable second-number possibilities remaining.

Now we are ready to start plugging in our combinations and cracking the lock. It does not matter which first number you start with. You can start with the first-number choice on the left and work right, start with the last first-number choice and work left, or start in the middle and work outward. I find it the easiest to start at the left and work right, but as long as you keep track of where you're at, it really doesn't matter. We will start with 1 as our first-number choice for simplicity's sake.

Give the dial a couple of spins to the right and stop at 1. By reading our table down, we find our first second-number choice to be 13. So rotate your dial to the left one full turn past 1 and stop at 13. We are now ready to utilize the characteristics of Principle 6 to determine the third number. Remember that this principle states that as we turn the dial back right, we can begin pulling up on the shackle without disrupting the placement of the other two numbers we have already set.

So with your table handy for reference, turn the dial to the right and stop four numbers away at the first gate you come to (9). Once here, give the shackle a quick pull. If it does not open, continue to the next gate (5), and give the shackle another quick pull. Continue this process until you get all the way back around to the initial second number you started with (13).

By utilizing the characteristics of Principle 4 and the same method used earlier to determine the second-number possibilities, we can reason that when we start to locate the third number it is less probable that the gate right after and before the second number will be the third number. For this reason you can initially skip these gates should you so desire. For example, after we stopped at 13 (as our second number) and began turning right, you can skip over the first gate (which was 9) and continue to the next gate (5) before starting to pull on the shackle. In the same respect, once you have rotated around to the next-to-last gate (21), you can stop and go to the next second-number possibility. This is simply a technique to save a couple of seconds on each rotation. (If this shortcut confuses you at all, disregard it. It does not hurt anything to make an attempt at every gate, it is simply a shortcut should you choose to utilize it. Also, keep in mind that even though it is a lot less probable that the third number falls within these parameters, it is still possible.)

If the lock did not open after trying all the third numbers, make a quick X through the second number you just attempted (13) and move on to the next second-number choice directly below it (17). Keeping the same first number (1), plug in your new second number (17) and begin the same technique as described earlier to find the third number. Turning the dial right to 13 and pulling out on the shackle, turning the dial to 9 and pulling out on the shackle, turning the dial to 5 and pulling out on the shackle, and so on.

Once you have plugged in the first two numbers, rotating and pulling to find the third number should go very quickly. After a couple rotations, you should have the gate numbers memorized and should not have to refer to the table to tell you which numbers to stop on. Turn-pull, turn-pull; with a little practice you should find yourself becoming quite proficient at this procedure.

If the second second-number choice you attempted did not open the lock, proceed to the next one in line (21). Continue this process until you have tried all the second-number choices in that column. Once completed, move on to the next first-number possibility (5). You will now be using 5 as your first number for the next iteration. Use the same sequence of steps as before, starting with 17, then 21, 25, 29, and lastly 33 as your second-number choices. If none of these combinations has opened the lock, continue working across the table in the same manner until it does.

By crossing out the numbers as you try them, you will be better able to keep track of where you are and save valuable time by not having to redial numbers you've already attempted.

If the lock doesn't open after attempting all first- and second-number combination possibilities in the table, go back and try the second and next-to-last second-number possibilities for each first-number possibility that we tentatively crossed out earlier. For example, using 1 as your first number, try 9 and 33 and your second-number choices, and so on down the line. (It is highly improbable that these numbers will be your second number. In the hundreds of locks that I have opened, I have only had it occur a couple of times. It is more likely to occur in Master Locks than in American locks. Anything is possible though, so don't rule it out.)

If you've tried all possible first- and second-number possibilities and the lock has still not opened, one of two things has happened.

1. You made some mistake in calculating the gate locations, or a gate location. Recheck your work, being very attentive to the feel of each gate and figuring their centermost point. Also make sure you did not simply copy down the wrong gate number on your paper. Writing down 15 instead of 17 could definitely make a difference.

2. You made an error while dialing. That is to say, in your quest for speed or simply by mistake, you over- or undershot a number by enough that you were not in the desired gate location and thus the lock would not open.

The only advice I can give here is to start over and be more careful to land more accurately on the desired numbers. This technique *will* open your combination padlock. So if for some reason your lock does not open after attempting all combination possibilities, ensure your gate locations are correct and pay more attention to the accuracy that you turn the dial.

IN REVIEW

1. Accurately find the center of the gates and record them

2.   Complete the table

3.   Tentatively cross out the first and last two rows

4.   Start plugging in the first and second numbers on the table

5.   Pull out on the shackle at every gate all the way back around the dial to determine the third gate

6.   Continue this process down the column

7.   Continue this process with a new first number if it fails to open

8.   If it still fails to open after attempting all numbers in the most probable range, extend the probable range to include those numbers tentatively crossed out earlier

With a little practice, it should only take about 20 minutes to accurately attempt all the combination possibilities designated on the table. So even if the combination is the last one in the formula you attempt, it should still take less than 20 minutes to open. If you get lucky and the combination lies in the first set of numbers you choose to start with, it will take only minutes.

Twelve-Gate Locks

As I touched on earlier, some combination padlocks will have more than 10 gates. Master Lock's combination locks are a good example of this, as they contain 12 gates (see Figure 3). More gates means more combination possibilities. It is basically an added security feature. For us, however, it is just a time-constraint feature. Our technique will still work as effectively, it will simply take a couple of additional minutes to open.

There are a couple of small points that deserve discussion in relation to our technique and the differences between the 10- and 12-gate locks. After experimenting with different lock brands, you will soon become familiar with which brands have 10 gates and which have 12. It is not mandatory that you know this before you begin working on the lock, however, because when you start the first step (which is finding the gate locations), you will immediately figure it out.

As you are finding and recording your gates, you will start to notice a few differences. The first one is that there is less range of motion between the gate walls. That is to say, when you find the gate and are turning the dial back and forth to determine its left and right limits, the dial does not turn as far and encompasses fewer numbers. Before, the dial would usually

Figure 3: Rear view (cutaway) of a 12-gate lock.

turn within two numbers, so we would simply take the middle of the two numbers for our center point. Now, you will find that the dial will only turn within one, or sometimes less then one number. To ensure accuracy in determining the centermost point of the gate, you may have to use 1/2 numbers.

You will also notice that the gate's center points are not perfectly spaced numbers as before. There is a pattern that emerges, however, as will be explained in greater detail later. Taking a Master Lock combination padlock as our example, we find the gates to be:

2½-6-9-12½-16-19-22½-26-29-32½-36-39

Your gates may be slightly different, but the concept remains the same. The gates from our 10-gate lock were evenly spaced every four numbers; while this is not the case with the 12-gate locks, the procedure and technique we used earlier remains constant. Using this set of numbers as our first numbers, continue to fill out the table in the same manner as performed earlier (see Table 3).

Tentatively cross out the first and last two rows as described earlier as well, leaving the most probable second-number choices (see Table 4). The technique from this point is exactly the same as before. Plug in a first number, continue down the second-number choices, and rotate the dial back around while pulling out on the shackle to find the third number.

As explained, there will be several more combination possibilities, resulting in extra time to try the additional numbers. With practice though, it should still take less than 30 minutes

1st No. Possibilities

2 ½	6	9	12 ½	16	19	22 ½	26	29	32 ½	36	39
6	9	12 ½	16	19	22 ½	26	29	32 ½	36	39	2 ½
9	12 ½	16	19	22 ½	26	29	32 ½	36	39	2 ½	6
12 ½	16	19	22 ½	26	29	32 ½	36	39	2 ½	6	9
16	19	22 ½	26	29	32 ½	36	39	2 ½	6	9	12 ½
19	22 ½	26	29	32 ½	36	39	2 ½	6	9	12 ½	16
22 ½	26	29	32 ½	36	39	2 ½	6	9	12 ½	16	19
26	29	32 ½	36	39	2 ½	6	9	12 ½	16	19	22 ½
29	32 ½	36	39	2 ½	6	9	12 ½	16	19	22 ½	26
32 ½	36	39	2 ½	6	9	12 ½	16	19	22 ½	26	29
36	39	2 ½	6	9	12 ½	16	19	22 ½	26	29	32 ½
39	2 ½	6	9	12 ½	16	19	22 ½	26	29	32 ½	36

2nd No. Possibilities (left-side label)

TABLE 3

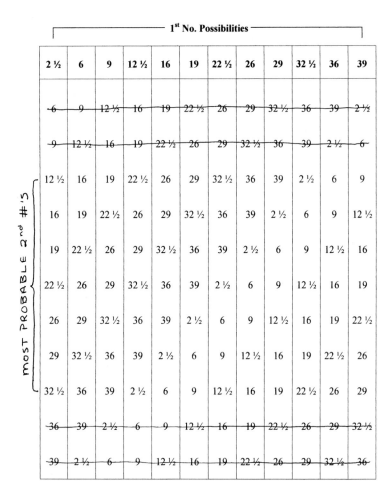

MOST PROBABLE 2nd #'S

1st No. Possibilities											
2 ½	6	9	12 ½	16	19	22 ½	26	29	32 ½	36	39
6	9	12 ½	16	19	22 ½	26	29	32 ½	36	39	2 ½
9	12 ½	16	19	22 ½	26	29	32 ½	36	39	2 ½	6
12 ½	16	19	22 ½	26	29	32 ½	36	39	2 ½	6	9
16	19	22 ½	26	29	32 ½	36	39	2 ½	6	9	12 ½
19	22 ½	26	29	32 ½	36	39	2 ½	6	9	12 ½	16
22 ½	26	29	32 ½	36	39	2 ½	6	9	12 ½	16	19
26	29	32 ½	36	39	2 ½	6	9	12 ½	16	19	22 ½
29	32 ½	36	39	2 ½	6	9	12 ½	16	19	22 ½	26
32 ½	36	39	2 ½	6	9	12 ½	16	19	22 ½	26	29
36	39	2 ½	6	9	12 ½	16	19	22 ½	26	29	32 ½
39	2 ½	6	9	12 ½	16	19	22 ½	26	29	32 ½	36

TABLE 4

to attempt all the combinations if needed. If you are luckier than I am, the combination will be in one of the first sets of numbers you start with.

One-Gate
Locks

Now let's take a look at a combination padlock that's a little bit different than the ones we've been working with. There are several companies that have come out with a combination lock that has only one gate—the true gate. Figure 4 shows the back of a Master Lock, and you'll notice that the third wheel is almost completely round except for one gate.

Figure 5 shows the back of a different series Master Lock (1500D). (This series from Master Lock is identical to those from Excel.) We notice the third wheel of this lock is similar to the one in Figure 4 but with a small angled notch cut out just to the left of the gate. This may initially appear to cause a problem with our formula, but it will simply call for a change in direction. We will, in essence, simply be working backwards instead of forwards.

We'll start as before by trying to locate the gates but first, there is something that needs to be touched on and emphasized about the lock in Figure 5. It is important that when locating the gate, you pay close attention to the friction of the dial and the gate limits. It is possible to misconstrue the small angled notch to the gate's left as the gate itself if you are rushing or not being careful. There should be a three-number area of movement with definite limits when you hit the gate. There is more friction when you locate the notch and, though it may initially seem that there is a right and left limit that resembles a gate, if you firmly turn the dial rights it will slip out of the angled notch. This is not something that should cause doubt or concern; once you have tried one of these types of locks and are aware of the way they work, you will have no problem in determining the true gate.

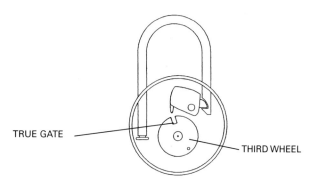

Figure 4: Rear view (cutaway) of a one-gate lock.

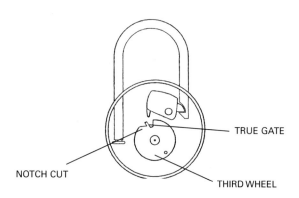

Figure 5: Rear view (cutaway) of a one-gate lock with notch cut.

Once you have located the gate location and its centermost point, this will be the third number in the combination. Record it. As touched on earlier, there is a pattern to the location of the gates in locks with 12 gates. It may not be as pretty as in the 10-gate locks (every four numbers), but there is still a pattern and you'll need to understand it.

Starting at 0, the first gate will lie between 0 and 3. The second gate will be +3½ numbers of the first gate (whatever it may be), the third gate will be +3 numbers of the second gate, the fourth gate will be +3½, the fifth gate +3½, the sixth gate +3, the seventh gate +3½, the eighth gate +3½, the ninth gate +3, the tenth gate +3½, the eleventh gate +3½, the twelfth gate + 3, and from the last gate to the first gate should be +3½. A simple breakdown looks like this, with X being the first gate location number:

GATES

1=X
2=X+3½
3=+3
4=+3½
5=+3½
6=+3
7=+3½
8=+3½
9=+3
10=+3½
11=+3½
12=+3

As you probably noticed, there is a pattern. Two 3½s followed by a 3, two 3½s followed by a 3, etc. In the 10-gate locks, gates are every fourth number, which you can determine by simply dividing the amount of numbers on the dial (40) by the number of gates (10). To determine the number/gate ratio for the 12-gate locks, we use the same equation with a slight variation. If you divide 40 by 12 you get 3.33, and since it would be extremely difficult to break our trial numbers down that fine, we will simply round up or down to the nearest ½ number. This process gives us the pattern we will use for 12-gate locks. Now let's plug in some numbers so we can see exactly how it works. We will use the number 1 as our first gate location. Using the above technique, we find the rest of the gates to be the following:

GATES

1=1
2=4½
3=7½
4=11
5=14½
6=17½
7=21
8=24½
9=27½
10=31
11=34½
12=37½

As stated earlier, the first-gate number ranges from 0 to three, which means there are seven first-gate possibilities within this range (0, ½, 1, 1½, 2, 2½, and 3). Any gate found after three will be gate two. Now let's take the seven first-gate possibilities, plug in our formula to determine their remaining respective gates, and record them.

FIRST-GATE POSSIBILITIES

Row 1: 0   3½   6½   10   13½   16½   20   23½   26½   30   33½ 36½

Row 2: ½   4   7   10½   14   17   20½   24   27   30½   34   37

Row 3: 1   4½   7½   11   14½   17½   21   24½   27½   31   34½ 37½

Row 4: 1½   5   8   11½   15   18   21½   25   28   31½   35   38

Row 5: 2   5½   8½   12   15½   18½   22   25½   28½ 32   35½ 38½

Row 6: 2½ 6   9   12½ 16   19   22½ 26   29   32½ 36   39

Row 7: 3   6½ 9½ 13   16½ 19½ 23   26½ 29½ 33   36½ 39½

It is not absolutely necessary that you perfectly understand how we arrived at the above table, only that you understand how to reference and use the table. This table represents all the different sets of gates found on a 12-gate combination lock; it can be used as an aid while determining the previous 12-gate combination formula, but is not mandatory since we can determine the gates by feel. (We will need this table as a reference with the one-gate locks, however, since we are unable to accomplish this task by feel since they have only one gate.)

This table will now be used as a reference in determining which set of gates we will use to find our combination. At this point we know:

1. The location of one gate

2. That this gate represents the third number in the combination

3. All the different gate location possibilities of the lock.

This is all the information we need. The next step is to record the number of the gate location we can find. We will use 19 as an example, as being the most accurately determined centermost point of our one gate. We then go to our table and find the number 19 in Row 6. This becomes the set of gate numbers that will be used in our equation.

The numbers in Row 6 represent the 12 first-number possibilities in our combination, just as before. So now we set up our new table, putting these numbers at the top as the first-number possibilities, and fill in the remainder of the table in the same fashion as before (see Table 5).

Once accomplished, we can again refer to our lock principles and tentatively cross out the first and last two rows. Since we know the last number is 19, we can cross out every 19 that appears in our table as a second-number choice, because the second and third number obviously can't be the same. Using the same rationalization, we can also tentatively cross out the numbers on either side of 19 (16 and 22½) as second-number possibilities. We can then use Principle 5 (high-low-high) to find the most probable first numbers to start with.

Knowing the last number to be 19, we can determine the most probable first numbers to be 9 through 29. This range of numbers encompasses the known last number (19) and the next three numbers on either side of it (9, 12½, 16, 22½, 26, and 29). Table 6 shows a table with the least-probable number combinations crossed out, and our most probable numbers, or sweet spot, remaining.

Now we are ready to begin. You can start with any first number in the most probable range, but I suggest trying 19 as your first number and working your way out. Using a similar technique as before, begin by dialing 19 as your first number.

Going down the column, the technique is basically the same as before except for one small change. We will start with 19 as our first-number choice. Once dialed, go down the column and plug in your second number (29) in the same manner as before. Now that we know the last number, there is no need to pull out on the shackle at every gate (especially since there are no other gates), so simply plug in 19 as the third number and try the combination. If it does not open, go to your next second-number choice (32½) and try 19 as your third number again. Continue this process until all the second-number choices in that column are exhausted, and move on to another first-number choice (16 or 22½ would be the next most probable).

If after you have tried all the first-number combination possibilities in the sweet spot without success, extend the probable range to include those number possibilities that we tentatively crossed out earlier. I would suggest trying the first-number combinations that were deemed less probable first, then moving to extend the second-number possibilities.

1st No. Possibilities

2 ½	6	9	12 ½	16	19	22 ½	26	29	32 ½	36	39
6	9	12 ½	16	19	22 ½	26	29	32 ½	36	39	2 ½
9	12 ½	16	19	22 ½	26	29	32 ½	36	39	2 ½	6
12 ½	16	19	22 ½	26	29	32 ½	36	39	2 ½	6	9
16	19	22 ½	26	29	32 ½	36	39	2 ½	6	9	12 ½
19	22 ½	26	29	32 ½	36	39	2 ½	6	9	12 ½	16
22 ½	26	29	32 ½	36	39	2 ½	6	9	12 ½	16	19
26	29	32 ½	36	39	2 ½	6	9	12 ½	16	19	22 ½
29	32 ½	36	39	2 ½	6	9	12 ½	16	19	22 ½	26
32 ½	36	39	2 ½	6	9	12 ½	16	19	22 ½	26	29
36	39	2 ½	6	9	12 ½	16	19	22 ½	26	29	32 ½
39	2 ½	6	9	12 ½	16	19	22 ½	26	29	32 ½	36

2nd No. Possibilities

TABLE 5

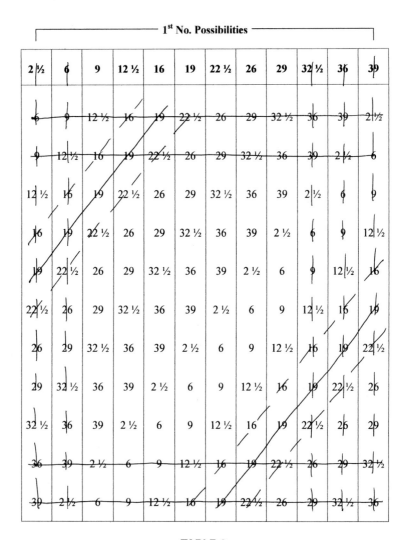

1st No. Possibilities											
2½	6	9	12½	16	19	22½	26	29	32½	36	39
6	9	12½	16	19	22½	26	29	32½	36	39	2½
9	12½	16	19	22½	26	29	32½	36	39	2½	6
12½	16	19	22½	26	29	32½	36	39	2½	6	9
16	19	22½	26	29	32½	36	39	2½	6	9	12½
19	22½	26	29	32½	36	39	2½	6	9	12½	16
22½	26	29	32½	36	39	2½	6	9	12½	16	19
26	29	32½	36	39	2½	6	9	12½	16	19	22½
29	32½	36	39	2½	6	9	12½	16	19	22½	26
32½	36	39	2½	6	9	12½	16	19	22½	26	29
36	39	2½	6	9	12½	16	19	22½	26	29	32½
39	2½	6	9	12½	16	19	22½	26	29	32½	36

TABLE 6

This all may sound somewhat complicated at first, especially if you have never dealt with combination lock manipulation before, but do not make it harder than it is.

IN REVIEW

1. Accurately find the center of the gate and record it

2. Use the table to find which set of numbers it falls into

3. Using that set of numbers as your first-number possibilities, complete the table

4. Tentatively cross out:
    A: The first and last two rows
    B: The columns that are not within three gate locations to either side of the known last number
    C: The third number and the numbers on either side of it, wherever they appear throughout the second number possibilities

5. Using the numbers in the most probable range, start plugging in the first and second numbers

6. Plug in the third number, already known, as the last number in the combination

7. Continue this process down the column of second-number choices

8. Continue this process with a new first number if it fails to open

9. If it still fails to open after attempting all numbers in the most probable range, extend the probable range to include those numbers tentatively crossed out earlier

It is just like anything else. The more you practice and work with it, the more proficient you will become in mastering the technique.

Conclusion

Lock companies are continually coming out with various new and altered designs. The techniques I have discussed throughout this book will aid you in opening any combination padlock on the market. As new locks are introduced, however, it might be necessary to crack one open and explore its new characteristics if you are not having the desired success with the formulas described here.

The designs of combination padlocks as a whole have not changed that much over the last 25 years or so, and I would not expect any drastic change in the future. For one thing, there is only so much you can do with a combination padlock to increase its security measures. There have been some changes—mainly small alterations—so keep this in mind in your exploration for entry.

Additional tables and illustrations have been added on the following pages for your use and reference.

Appendix A:
Ten-Gate Locks

0	4	8	12	16	20	24	28	32	36
4	8	12	16	20	24	28	32	36	0
8	12	16	20	24	28	32	36	0	4
12	16	20	24	28	32	36	0	4	8
16	20	24	28	32	36	0	4	8	12
20	24	28	32	36	0	4	8	12	16
24	28	32	36	0	4	8	12	16	20
28	32	36	0	4	8	12	16	20	24
32	36	0	4	8	12	16	20	24	28
36	0	4	8	12	16	20	24	28	32

1\2	4 ½	8 ½	12 ½	16 ½	20 ½	24 ½	28 ½	32 ½	36 ½
4 ½	8 ½	12 ½	16 ½	20 ½	24 ½	28 ½	32 ½	36 ½	½
8 ½	12 ½	16 ½	20 ½	24 ½	28 ½	32 ½	36 ½	½	4 ½
12 ½	16 ½	20 ½	24 ½	28 ½	32 ½	36 ½	½	4 ½	8 ½
16 ½	20 ½	24 ½	28 ½	32 ½	36 ½	½	4 ½	8 ½	12 ½
20 ½	24 ½	28 ½	32 ½	36 ½	½	4 ½	8 ½	12 ½	16 ½
24 ½	28 ½	32 ½	36 ½	½	4 ½	8 ½	12 ½	16 ½	20 ½
28 ½	32 ½	36 ½	½	4 ½	8 ½	12 ½	16 ½	20 ½	24 ½
32 ½	36 ½	½	4 ½	8 ½	12 ½	16 ½	20 ½	24 ½	28 ½
36 ½	½	4 ½	8 ½	12 ½	16 ½	20 ½	24 ½	28 ½	32 ½

1	5	9	13	17	21	25	29	33	37
5	9	13	17	21	25	29	33	37	1
9	13	17	21	25	29	33	37	1	5
13	17	21	25	29	33	37	1	5	9
17	21	25	29	33	37	1	5	9	13
21	25	29	33	37	1	5	9	13	17
25	29	33	37	1	5	9	13	17	21
29	33	37	1	5	9	13	17	21	25
33	37	1	5	9	13	17	21	25	29
37	1	5	9	13	17	21	25	29	33

1 ½	5 ½	9 ½	13 ½	17 ½	21 ½	25 ½	29 ½	33 ½	37 ½
5 ½	9 ½	13 ½	17 ½	21 ½	25 ½	29 ½	33 ½	37 ½	1 ½
9 ½	13 ½	17 ½	21 ½	25 ½	29 ½	33 ½	37 ½	1 ½	5 ½
13 ½	17 ½	21 ½	25 ½	29 ½	33 ½	37 ½	1 ½	5 ½	9 ½
17 ½	21 ½	25 ½	29 ½	33 ½	37 ½	1 ½	5 ½	9 ½	13 ½
21 ½	25 ½	29 ½	33 ½	37 ½	1 ½	5 ½	9 ½	13 ½	17 ½
25 ½	29 ½	33 ½	37 ½	1 ½	5 ½	9 ½	13 ½	17 ½	21 ½
29 ½	33 ½	37 ½	1 ½	5 ½	9 ½	13 ½	17 ½	21 ½	25 ½
33 ½	37 ½	1 ½	5 ½	9 ½	13 ½	17 ½	21 ½	25 ½	29 ½
37 ½	1 ½	5 ½	9 ½	13 ½	17 ½	21 ½	25 ½	29 ½	33 ½

2	6	10	14	18	22	26	30	34	38
6	10	14	18	22	26	30	34	38	2
10	14	18	22	26	30	34	38	2	6
14	18	22	26	30	34	38	2	6	10
18	22	26	30	34	38	2	6	10	14
22	26	30	34	38	2	6	10	14	18
26	30	34	38	2	6	10	14	18	22
30	34	38	2	6	10	14	18	22	26
34	38	2	6	10	14	18	22	26	30
38	2	6	10	14	18	22	26	30	34

2 ½	6 ½	10 ½	14 ½	18 ½	22 ½	26 ½	30 ½	34 ½	38 ½
6 ½	10 ½	14 ½	18 ½	22 ½	26 ½	30 ½	34 ½	38 ½	2 ½
10 ½	14 ½	18 ½	22 ½	26 ½	30 ½	34 ½	38 ½	2 ½	6 ½
14 ½	18 ½	22 ½	26 ½	30 ½	34 ½	38 ½	2 ½	6 ½	10 ½
18 ½	22 ½	26 ½	30 ½	34 ½	38 ½	2 ½	6 ½	10 ½	14 ½
22 ½	26 ½	30 ½	34 ½	38 ½	2 ½	6 ½	10 ½	14 ½	18 ½
26 ½	30 ½	34 ½	38 ½	2 ½	6 ½	10 ½	14 ½	18 ½	22 ½
30 ½	34 ½	38 ½	2 ½	6 ½	10 ½	14 ½	18 ½	22 ½	26 ½
34 ½	38 ½	2 ½	6 ½	10 ½	14 ½	18 ½	22 ½	26 ½	30 ½
38 ½	2 ½	6 ½	10 ½	14 ½	18 ½	22 ½	26 ½	30 ½	34 ½

3	7	11	15	19	23	27	31	35	39
7	11	15	19	23	27	31	35	39	3
11	15	19	23	27	31	35	39	3	7
15	19	23	27	31	35	39	3	7	11
19	23	27	31	35	39	3	7	11	15
23	27	31	35	39	3	7	11	15	19
27	31	35	39	3	7	11	15	19	23
31	35	39	3	7	11	15	19	23	27
35	39	3	7	11	15	19	23	27	31
39	3	7	11	15	19	23	27	31	35

3 ½	7 ½	11 ½	15 ½	19 ½	23 ½	27 ½	31 ½	35 ½	39 ½
7 ½	11 ½	15 ½	19 ½	23 ½	27 ½	31 ½	35 ½	39 ½	3 ½
11 ½	15 ½	19 ½	23 ½	27 ½	31 ½	35 ½	39 ½	3 ½	7 ½
15 ½	19 ½	23 ½	27 ½	31 ½	35 ½	39 ½	3 ½	7 ½	11 ½
19 ½	23 ½	27 ½	31 ½	35 ½	39 ½	3 ½	7 ½	11 ½	15 ½
23 ½	27 ½	31 ½	35 ½	39 ½	3 ½	7 ½	11 ½	15 ½	19 ½
27 ½	31 ½	35 ½	39 ½	3 ½	7 ½	11 ½	15 ½	19 ½	23 ½
31 ½	35 ½	39 ½	3 ½	7 ½	11 ½	15 ½	19 ½	23 ½	27 ½
35 ½	39 ½	3 ½	7 ½	11 ½	15 ½	19 ½	23 ½	27 ½	31 ½
39 ½	3 ½	7 ½	11 ½	15 ½	19 ½	23 ½	27 ½	31 ½	35 ½

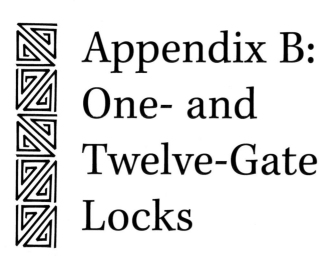

Appendix B: One- and Twelve-Gate Locks

FIRST GATE POSSIBILITIES

1:	0	3½	6½	10	13½	16½	20	23½	26½	30	33½	36½
2:	½	4	7	10½	14	17	20½	24	27	30½	34	37
3:	1	4½	7½	11	14½	17½	21	24½	27½	31	34½	37½
4:	1½	5	8	11½	15	18	21½	25	28	31½	35	38
5:	2	5½	8½	12	15½	18½	22	25½	28½	32	35½	38½
6:	2½	6	9	12½	16	19	22½	26	29	32½	36	39
7:	3	6½	9½	13	16½	19½	23	26½	29½	33	36½	39½

0	3 ½	6 ½	10	13 ½	16 ½	20	23 ½	26 ½	30	33 ½	36 ½
3 ½	6 ½	10	13 ½	16 ½	20	23 ½	26 ½	30	33 ½	36 ½	0
6 ½	10	13 ½	16 ½	20	23 ½	26 ½	30	33 ½	36 ½	0	3 ½
10	13 ½	16 ½	20	23 ½	26 ½	30	33 ½	36 ½	0	3 ½	6 ½
13 ½	16 ½	20	23 ½	26 ½	30	33 ½	36 ½	0	3 ½	6 ½	10
16 ½	20	23 ½	26 ½	30	33 ½	36 ½	0	3 ½	6 ½	10	13 ½
20	23 ½	26 ½	30	33 ½	36 ½	0	3 ½	6 ½	10	13 ½	16 ½
23 ½	26 ½	30	33 ½	36 ½	0	3 ½	6 ½	10	13 ½	16 ½	20
26 ½	30	33 ½	36 ½	0	3 ½	6 ½	10	13 ½	16 ½	20	23 ½
30	33 ½	36 ½	0	3 ½	6 ½	10	13 ½	16 ½	20	23 ½	26 ½
33 ½	36 ½	0	3 ½	6 ½	10	13 ½	16 ½	20	23 ½	26 ½	30
36 ½	0	3 ½	6 ½	10	13 ½	16 ½	20	23 ½	26 ½	30	33 ½

½	4	7	10 ½	14	17	20 ½	24	27	30 ½	34	37
4	7	10 ½	14	17	20 ½	24	27	30 ½	34	37	½
7	10 ½	14	17	20 ½	24	27	30 ½	34	37	½	4
10 ½	14	17	20 ½	24	27	30 ½	34	37	½	4	7
14	17	20 ½	24	27	30 ½	34	37	½	4	7	10 ½
17	20 ½	24	27	30 ½	34	37	½	4	7	10 ½	14
20 ½	24	27	30 ½	34	37	½	4	7	10 ½	14	17
24	27	30 ½	34	37	½	4	7	10 ½	14	17	20 ½
27	30 ½	34	37	½	4	7	10 ½	14	17	20 ½	24
30 ½	34	37	½	4	7	10 ½	14	17	20 ½	24	27
34	37	½	4	7	10 ½	14	17	20 ½	24	27	30 ½
37	½	4	7	10 ½	14	17	20 ½	24	27	30 ½	34

1	4½	7½	11	14½	17½	21	24½	27½	31	34½	37½
4½	7½	11	14½	17½	21	24½	27½	31	34½	37½	1
7½	11	14½	17½	21	24½	27½	31	34½	37½	1	4½
11	14½	17½	21	24½	27½	31	34½	37½	1	4½	7½
14½	17½	21	24½	27½	31	34½	37½	1	4½	7½	11
17½	21	24½	27½	31	34½	37½	1	4½	7½	11	14½
21	24½	27½	31	34½	37½	1	4½	7½	11	14½	17½
24½	27½	31	34½	37½	1	4½	7½	11	14½	17½	21
27½	31	34½	37½	1	4½	7½	11	14½	17½	21	24½
31	34½	37½	1	4½	7½	11	14½	17½	21	24½	27½
34½	37½	1	4½	7½	11	14½	17½	21	24½	27½	31
37½	1	4½	7½	11	14½	17½	21	24½	27½	31	34½

1 ½	5	8	11 ½	15	18	21 ½	25	28	31 ½	35	38
5	8	11 ½	15	18	21 ½	25	28	31 ½	35	38	1 ½
8	11 ½	15	18	21 ½	25	28	31 ½	35	38	1 ½	5
11 ½	15	18	21 ½	25	28	31 ½	35	38	1 ½	5	8
15	18	21 ½	25	28	31 ½	35	38	1 ½	5	8	11 ½
18	21 ½	25	28	31 ½	35	38	1 ½	5	8	11 ½	15
21 ½	25	28	31 ½	35	38	1 ½	5	8	11 ½	15	18
25	28	31 ½	35	38	1 ½	5	8	11 ½	15	18	21 ½
28	31 ½	35	38	1 ½	5	8	11 ½	15	18	21 ½	25
31 ½	35	38	1 ½	5	8	11 ½	15	18	21 ½	25	28
35	38	1 ½	5	8	11 ½	15	18	21 ½	25	28	31 ½
38	1 ½	5	8	11 ½	15	18	21 ½	25	28	31 ½	35

2	5 ½	8 ½	12	15 ½	18 ½	22	25 ½	28 ½	32	35 ½	38 ½
5 ½	8 ½	12 ½	15 ½	18 ½	22	25 ½	28 ½	32	35 ½	38 ½	2
8 ½	12	15 ½	18 ½	22	25 ½	28 ½	32	35 ½	38 ½	2	5 ½
12	15 ½	18 ½	22	25 ½	28 ½	32	35 ½	38 ½	2	5 ½	8 ½
15 ½	18 ½	22	25 ½	28 ½	32	35 ½	38 ½	2	5 ½	8 ½	12
18 ½	22	25 ½	28 ½	32	35 ½	38 ½	2	5 ½	8 ½	12	15 ½
22	25 ½	28 ½	32	35 ½	38 ½	2	5 ½	8 ½	12	15 ½	18 ½
25 ½	28 ½	32	35 ½	38 ½	2	5 ½	8 ½	12	15 ½	18 ½	22
28 ½	32	35 ½	38 ½	2	5 ½	8 ½	12	15 ½	18 ½	22	25 ½
32	35 ½	38 ½	2	5 ½	8 ½	12	15 ½	18 ½	22	25 ½	28 ½
35 ½	38 ½	2	5 ½	8 ½	12	15 ½	18 ½	22	25 ½	28 ½	32
38 ½	2	5 ½	8 ½	12	15 ½	18 ½	22	25 ½	28 ½	32	35 ½

2½	6	9	12½	16	19	22½	26	29	32½	36	39
6	9	12½	16	19	22½	26	29	32½	36	39	2½
9	12½	16	19	22½	26	29	32½	36	39	2½	6
12½	16	19	22½	26	29	32½	36	39	2½	6	9
16	19	22½	26	29	32½	36	39	2½	6	9	12½
19	22½	26	29	32½	36	39	2½	6	9	12½	16
22½	26	29	32½	36	39	2½	6	9	12½	16	19
26	29	32½	36	39	2½	6	9	12½	16	19	22½
29	32½	36	39	2½	6	9	12½	16	19	22½	26
32½	36	39	2½	6	9	12½	16	19	22½	26	29
36	39	2½	6	9	12½	16	19	22½	26	29	32½
39	2½	6	9	12½	16	19	22½	26	29	32½	36

3	6 ½	9 ½	13	16 ½	19 ½	23	26 ½	29 ½	33	36 ½	39 ½
6 ½	9 ½	13	16 ½	19 ½	23	26 ½	29 ½	33	36 ½	39 ½	3
9 ½	13	16 ½	19 ½	23	26 ½	29 ½	33	36 ½	39 ½	3	6 ½
13	16 ½	19 ½	23	26 ½	29 ½	33	36 ½	39 ½	3	6 ½	9 ½
16 ½	19 ½	23	26 ½	29 ½	33	36 ½	39 ½	3	6 ½	9 ½	13
19 ½	23	26 ½	29 ½	33	36 ½	39 ½	3	6 ½	9 ½	13	16 ½
23	26 ½	29 ½	33	36 ½	39 ½	3	6 ½	9 ½	13	16 ½	19 ½
26 ½	29 ½	33	36 ½	39 ½	3	6 ½	9 ½	13	16 ½	19 ½	23
29 ½	33	36 ½	39 ½	3	6 ½	9 ½	13	16 ½	19 ½	23	26 ½
33	36 ½	39 ½	3	6 ½	9 ½	13	16 ½	19 ½	23	26 ½	29 ½
36 ½	39 ½	3	6 ½	9 ½	13	16 ½	19 ½	23	26 ½	29 ½	33
39 ½	3	6 ½	9 ½	13	16 ½	19 ½	23	26 ½	29 ½	33	36 ½

Appendix C: Troubleshooting Techniques

Certain lock brands have a very small wheel-size differential between the first and second wheels and the third wheel. You will know when you come across one of these locks because you will probably be unable to find a clear-cut or recognizable gate. This will be more prominent in new or less-used locks. If you spin the dial while pulling up on the shackle and are unable to find a definite gate, proceed to the following technique:

First, loosen up the wheels. Put a little wear on the first and second wheels to make them slightly shift or move out of perfect alignment to create enough play to make additional contact with the third wheel. This can be done by pulling out on the shackle and repeatedly spinning the dial. After several turns, push the shackle back in and spin the dial a couple times while it doesn't have any resistance on it, then pull it back out and continue the process several more times.

Next, again apply outward pressure on the shackle and slowly turn the dial. At this point you should be able to feel, even if very slightly, small areas of friction while turning the dial clockwise. (We are still assuming that you are unable to clearly determine all ten or twelve gates.) These areas of friction could be from any or all of the wheels if it is a one-gate lock (though it is most likely you will only feel one), or from random gate notches on a ten– or twelve-gate lock. When you reach one of these areas of friction, it is unlikely that you will be able to move the dial left and find a specific left limit.

The area of friction is a slight brushing of the right side of the gate notch. After landing on one of these areas, you should be able to move the dial back left freely and then move it back right, "clicking" on the same resistance on the same spot. You will need to go through this process several times. If you find more than one, make note of the numbers they each lie on and record them each time you pass by. You may need to relieve the tension on the shackle every so often and then proceed.

If there is more than one area of resistance, choose the one that catches the strongest; this should be the true gate for wheel one. Check the dial number several times and ensure you have a gate area and not just a high wheel rubbing the area. Next, because you are at the extreme right limit of the gate, you will need to add one to it to receive a center mass position of the gate. Not all one-gate locks are technically twelve-gate locks so we could use the ten-gate tables and number sets to finish our manipulation process. While this would save time, without learning and memorizing every lock and lock revision it would be difficult to determine which one-gate lock was classified as a ten- or twelve-gate lock for manipulation purposes; thus, I encourage using the twelve-gate tables for all one-gate locks, or for any lock in which gates cannot be clearly determined. This process will work for both ten- and twelve-gate classifications, but ten-gate tables will not always work for twelve-gate locks.

When you have the possible first-gate number (and add one), find which row of numbers it falls into in Appendix B. You will use these as your first-gate possibilities and work through the manipulation process in the same fashion as if you were working on a twelve-gate lock. Even though it is much less probable, it is still possible that the gate you found and the number you used belongs to the second or third wheel. For this reason I recommend using the twelve-gate process and working forward instead of the one-gate process and working backward.